Out Order

Written by Karen Phelps
Illustrated by Rob Lang

Characters

Mrs Bhamra   **Narrator**

Guy Fawkes   **Brian**

Captain Cook   **Elizabeth I**

Narrator: Brian's class is at the museum, studying history. Everyone is walking past a thick black curtain with a sign that says, "Out of Order"… all the pupils, that is, except for Brian.

Brian: I wonder what's behind this curtain. It must be something really good if it's worn out from overuse!

Mrs Bhamra: Hurry up, everyone, and do stay together!

Narrator: Brian waits until Mrs Bhamra and the rest of the class disappear around the corner. Then he ducks behind the curtain.

Mrs Bhamra (*as if her voice is fading away*): I want you to search for information about the English Civil War. Also look for information on the early **emigrants** to Australia and New Zealand…

Brian (*to himself*):
This seems to be a room full of models of famous people in history. This is the coolest exhibit in the whole museum. I wonder why they've closed it off?

Narrator: Beside each of the models there is a button.

Brian: I wonder what will happen if I press the button next to this guy with the funny hat…

Guy Fawkes: Hello, Guy Fawkes is my name. I tried to **assassinate** King James I, but I was caught in the act and punished. My name lives on, though. Every year people celebrate Guy Fawkes Night by lighting bonfires and setting off fireworks.

Brian: Wow, this is really cool! I wonder who this woman standing next to him is.

Narrator: Brian presses another button.

Elizabeth I: I'm Elizabeth I, Queen of England. I was crowned on the 15th of January, 1559.

Brian (*to himself*): Wasn't she the queen who was famous for her bad temper?

Elizabeth I: How dare you suggest such a thing, young man? I am very good-natured once you get to know me. I did once throw a slipper at one of my royal advisors, Francis Walsingham, but he deserved it!

Brian: Hold on – are you talking to me?

Elizabeth I: I most certainly am, young man! You should be careful – another comment like that and I might send you to The Tower!

Brian: But how can you do that, you're not real… are you?

Elizabeth I: Too late to be worrying about that now, my boy. Didn't you read the sign?

Guy Fawkes: We've been hoping someone would ignore that sign and come in here.

Elizabeth I:	Mind your manners, Mr Fawkes! I haven't finished yet. As I was saying, I was crowned Queen of England. Under my rule, England repelled the attack of the mighty Spanish Armada.
Brian:	Sounds like a tough battle!
Elizabeth I:	And that's not all I had to deal with. In 1587, I ordered the **execution** of my own cousin, Mary, Queen of Scots.
Brian:	Talk about family feuding!
Narrator:	Sparks arc across wires on the floor.

Captain Cook: Hello, I'm Captain Cook. I am an explorer, navigator, and **cartographer**.

Brian: Wait a minute! I didn't even push your button! What's going on?

Captain Cook: I went on three voyages to the South Pacific over 200 years ago. It is said that I was the first British explorer to discover the east coast of Australia and the Hawaiian islands, and the first explorer to find and map New Zealand.

Brian: I bet you had some pretty wild adventures!

Guy Fawkes: If you're impressed by that, you should hear what *I* did! On the 5th of November, 1605, I sneaked into a cellar below the Houses of Parliament and, together with some associates, planted barrels of gunpowder. We tried to blow up the building.

Brian: But doesn't that make you a criminal?

Guy Fawkes: Well, I believed King James had **reneged** on his promise to stop **persecuting** Catholics. I felt strongly that he should be punished for this.

Brian: It sounds kind of complicated.

Guy Fawkes: History often is. I thought what I did was right, but I was tortured and put to death. Many families lit bonfires all over England to celebrate the fact that the King had survived my attempt on his life. People keep the tradition up to this very day.

Elizabeth I: I don't know what you're boasting about, Guy. You should be ashamed of what you did!

Captain Cook: And it's nothing compared to sailing across the South Pacific!

Guy Fawkes: That's just what I'd expect you to say, Captain Cook. Anyway, I heard that you weren't actually the first person to discover Australia or New Zealand.

Captain Cook: Brian, don't listen to him. He's nothing more than a common criminal who wears a funny hat. Hello, I'm Captain Cook!

Elizabeth I: I'm more important than both of you put together. People say I am the most admired monarch of all. They call my reign "The Golden Age".

Captain Cook: Hello, I'm Captain Cook... Hello, I'm Captain Cook...

Guy Fawkes: Still talking about yourself, I see!

Elizabeth I: Signing death warrants was more fun than listening to you two. To The Tower for you both, I say!

Brian (*to himself*):
Oh no, the models must be **malfunctioning**!

Narrator: Brian starts searching for a way to turn the models off.

Elizabeth I: Don't even think about trying to switch us off, young man! The buttons don't work.

Guy Fawkes: That's why the sign said "Out of Order"!

Captain Cook: Hello, I'm Captain Cook...

Guy Fawkes: What's that boy up to now?

Elizabeth I: Oh, no! He's found the plug! Quick! Stop him!

Captain Cook: Hello, I'm Captain Cook...

Elizabeth I and Guy Fawkes: Be quiet!

Narrator: With all his strength, Brian pulls the plug out of the wall. There is a burst of sparks.

Captain Cook (*slowing down*): H-e-llo... I'm... Cap... tain... Co...

Elizabeth I (*slowing down*): Wait... we... still... have...

Guy Fawkes (*slowing down*): ...so... much... to... sayyy...

Narrator: The models droop over like rag dolls. Brian rushes back through the curtains.

Mrs Bhamra (*gradually getting louder*): That concludes our visit to this fascinating museum. The bus will be leaving in ten minutes.

Narrator: Mrs Bhamra and the rest of Brian's class are leaving the museum. Brian slips in behind the last person.

Mrs Bhamra: Well class, I hope this trip to the museum has helped bring history alive for you. As you can see, history is not just something set in the past. History is made every day – it might start with something little...

Brian: …such as hatching a plot to address something you think is wrong, like Guy Fawkes did.

Mrs Bhamra (*surprised*): That's correct, Brian – excellent connection! Or, it could be something with the significance of…

Brian: …defeating the Spanish Armada, like Queen Elizabeth I, or exploring the South Pacific, like Captain Cook!

Mrs Bhamra (*impressed*): Right again, Brian. I'm glad you've been paying attention. The important question to ask yourself is… how will *you* make history?